Mammals

BY MICHELLE LEVINE

amicus
high interest

Amicus High Interest is an imprint of Amicus
P.O. Box 1329, Mankato, MN 56002
www.amicuspublishing.us

Library of Congress Cataloging-in-Publication Data
Levine, Michelle, author.
 Mammals / Michelle Levine.
    pages cm. — (Animal Kingdom)
 Summary: "An introduction to what characteristics animals in
the mammal animal class have and how they fit into the animal
kingdom"— Provided by publisher.
 Audience: K to grade 3.
 Includes bibliographical references and index.
 ISBN 978-1-60753-475-4 (library binding) —
 ISBN 978-1-60753-622-2 (ebook)
 1. Mammals—Juvenile literature. I. Title.
 QL706.2.L48 2015
 599—dc23
                                        2013031391

Editor: Wendy Dieker
Series Designer: Kathleen Petelinsek
Book Designer: Heather Dreisbach
Photo Researcher: Kurtis Kinneman

Photo Credits: Minden Pictures/SuperStock, cover; Biosphoto/
SuperStock, 5; Laura Romin & Larry Dalton/Alamy, 6; Jacinto
Yoder/Shutterstock, 9; Vince Burton/Alamy, 11; AfriPics.
com/Alamy, 13; Don Johnston/Alamy, 14; Anette Holmberg/
Shutterstock, 17; Martin Harvey/Alamy, 18; Premium Stock
Photography GmbH/Alamy, 20; K.A.Willis/Shutterstock, 23;
Ernie Janes/Alamy, 24-25; defotoberg/Shutterstock, 26; All
Canada Photos/Alamy, 29

Printed in the United States of America at Corporate Graphics
in North Mankato, Minnesota.

10 9 8 7 6 5 4 3 2 1

Table of Contents

What Is a Mammal?

Roar! A lion call warns an enemy. Splash! A whale swims in the sea. Crunch! A squirrel bites an acorn. Boing! A kangaroo jumps along. These animals do not all look alike. And they do not live in the same places. But they belong to the same animal **class**. They are all mammals.

A whale is not a fish. It is a mammal that lives in water.

A newborn elephant stays with its mother. It will drink her milk.

 Q Are people mammals?

Mammals are alike in special ways. One way is how they feed their young. Mother mammals make milk for their babies. No other animal does this. Mammals are also **warm-blooded**. They make their own heat. So their body temperature stays the same. It does not change in hot or cold weather.

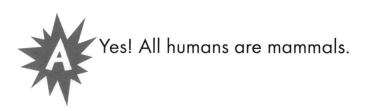
Yes! All humans are mammals.

Mammals also have hair or fur. But some only have a little hair. Others have it only when they are young.

Most mammals also have four limbs. You have two arms and two legs. Many other mammals have four legs. At the ends are paws or hooves.

 Do all mammals have arms or legs?

**Sloths have long hair
and long limbs.**

A No. Water mammals don't. They have flippers.
Bats have two legs and two wings.

Eat or Be Eaten

Chomp! A wolf eats its meal. Mammals eat different kinds of food. Some are like the wolf. They are **carnivores**. They hunt and eat other animals. They use their claws to catch **prey**. They use their sharp teeth to eat it. Lions and otters are other carnivores.

Wolves are mammals that hunt.

Munch! A hippo chews some grass. Mammals such as hippos and zebras are **herbivores**. They eat only plants. Their teeth are made for this kind of food. Their bottom teeth are flat for grinding.

Mammals such as humans and bears are **omnivores**. They eat both plants and animals. Other mammals are **scavengers**. They eat dead animals.

Hippos spend time in water. But they go to the land to eat grass.

This rabbit hides in a hole. But it can run fast if it's in danger.

 How does a skunk stay safe?

Most mammals also have **predators**.
So how do they stay safe? Their color
helps. Many of them blend into their
surroundings. They also have strong legs.
They run and hide from danger. Or they
climb up trees. Others use their claws.
They dig tunnels underground. Or they
fight their predators.

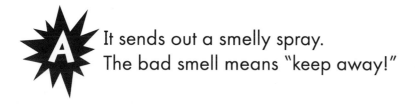 It sends out a smelly spray.
The bad smell means "keep away!"

Living on Land and in Water

Mammals have **adapted** to live almost everywhere on Earth. Polar bears live in icy places. Their thick fur keeps them warm. Camels live in dry deserts. Their bodies need less water than ours do. Whales and dolphins have smooth bodies for swimming. The bodies of other mammals are made for climbing or running.

 Do any mammals fly?

Polar bears have thick fur and a layer of fat. They can live in very cold places.

Some mammals can glide from tree to tree. But bats are the only ones that truly fly.

Warthogs have a strong sense of smell to find food buried in the dirt.

18

Mammals use their senses to survive.
Many land mammals have powerful
noses. They can smell food from far away.
They can also smell their enemies. Water
mammals have powerful hearing. They
hear sounds we can't. Mammals have big
brains too. They can learn new skills. And
they can think fast to stay safe. That also
helps them survive.

A male red deer calls out to find a
mate. Females follow the sound.

Making Babies

Male and female mammals come together to **mate**. Many mate in spring or early summer. Others mate year round. They have different ways of finding each other. Deer call out to each other. Other mammals send out a special smell. And some monkeys show off their colorful bodies. These are all messages. They mean, "Let's get together!"

Most mammal babies grow inside their mothers. Then the mother gives birth to a live animal. Mice are born after just a few weeks. Elephants are born after 18 to 22 months! But all mammal mothers **nurse** their young. That is, they feed their babies their own milk. Some of them nurse for weeks. Others nurse for months or years.

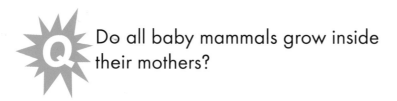

Do all baby mammals grow inside their mothers?

A kangaroo carries its baby in its pouch.

Most do. But some, like kangaroos, finish growing in their mother's pouch. A few mammals, such as the platypus, hatch from eggs!

23

Young mammals take a long time to grow up. They stay with their mothers for months or years. Mammal mothers are good teachers. They teach how to find food. They also teach how to stay safe. No other animal mothers teach in this way.

Baby baboons stay with their mother for 18 months.

Big horses help farmers pull tools and machines.

 How many kinds of mammals are on Earth?

Mammals in the World

Mammals such as cats and dogs make good pets. Larger mammals help people in other ways. Donkeys and camels carry people from place to place. Horses help out on some farms.

Mammals are also an important source of food. Humans and other mammals eat mammals. So do other kinds of animals.

Up to 5,000.

Many mammals are in danger of going **extinct**. Farms and cities destroy wild places. The animals lose their homes. They lose their source of food and water. This has happened to the American bison. But people are working to protect mammals and their homes. That way, they can live on for years to come.

American bison almost died out. Their herds are growing again.

Glossary

adapt To change in order to survive.

carnivore A meat–eating animal.

class A group of animals that share similar characteristics.

extinct Died out.

herbivore A plant–eating animal.

mate To come together to make babies.

nurse To feed a baby milk from its mother.

omnivore An animal that eats both plants and animals.

predator An animal that hunts other animals.

prey An animal that is food for another animal.

scavenger An animal that eats dead animals.

warm-blooded To be able to make body heat and keep the same body temperature.

Read More

Cleary, Brian P. *Dolphin, Fox, Hippo and Ox: What Is a Mammal?* Minneapolis: Millbrook Press, 2013.

Salas, Laura Purdie. *Mammals: Hairy, Milk-Making Animals.* Minneapolis: Picture Window Books, 2010.

Silverman, Buffy. *Do You Know about Mammals?* Minneapolis: Lerner, 2010.

Websites

Creature Feature: National Geographic Kids
http://kids.nationalgeographic.com/kids/animals/creaturefeature/

Enchanted Learning: Mammals
http://www.enchantedlearning.com/subjects/mammals/Classroom.shtml

San Diego Zoo: Kids: Mammals
http://kids.sandiegozoo.org/animals/mammals

Index

About the Author

Michelle Levine has written and edited many nonfiction books for children. She loves learning about new things—like mammals—and sharing what she's learned with her readers. She lives in St. Paul, Minnesota.